An American Celebration

SAMPLER PUBLICATIONS
St. Charles, Illinois

Country Sampler's Christmas Gatherings: *An American Celebration*

Library of Congress Catalog Card Number: 91-065668
ISBN: 0-944493-05-X

Editors:
Joanne Lowery
Debra Anton

Art Director:
Jill Haack

Crafts Editor:
Susan Laity Price

Food Editor:
Grace Howaniec

Photo Stylists:
Sally Enstad
Carol Schalla
Sue Worthley
Food: Heather Hill

Studio Photography:
Dick Kaplan
Bob Gibbs

SAMPLER PUBLICATIONS, INC.

CEO and Executive Publisher:
Mark A. Nickel

President:
H. Russell Weller

Vice President, Group Publisher:
Margaret B. Kernan

Editorial Director:
Steve Slack

Executive Art Director/Production Manager:
Daniel Zock

Director of Manufacturing:
William D. Lowry

Controller:
John Salmon

C E L E B R A T E

Every year in homes across America Christmas becomes the expression of all we hold dear: family, friends, beauty and sharing. We open our homes and our hearts to loved ones as we exchange handmade keepsakes and serve homebaked goodies by the magical light of a resplendent tree. Welcome, we say.

For weeks beforehand we make lists, collect ideas, sort through treasured ornaments, search out favorite cookie recipes, and get busy. From hours of fixing and fussing, our homes take on their holiday best, dressed up in pine and sparkle, fragrant with sugar and spices. Finally the gifts are wrapped, the cookie tins brimming, the mantel graced with stockings. On a snowy Christmas Eve, the doorbell rings and the welcome begins.

Christmas is a collection of endless variations on this theme — there is no one American way to celebrate the holidays. Each family has a different box of precious decorations and a different set of traditions familiar since childhood. In a country as diverse as ours, many families choose to follow ethnic customs or regional variations, or they prefer a certain kind of beauty that blends with their lifestyle and decor. That's why we at Sampler Publications offer you four styles of Christmas decorating, food, and crafts to inspire you. Find your style, or try a new one. However you choose to wish your family and friends a Merry Christmas this year, the spirit of welcome will fill your home.

Country Christmas speaks of friends and relatives gathered 'round a kitchen table, sharing the joy of America's most important holiday season. Surrounded by laughter, comfort-filled food, and decorations reminiscent of times gone by, country families celebrate the pleasures of hearth and home.

They come home to red-white-and-blue ornaments that express the enduring American values of freedom and brotherhood, to informal caroling parties and rooms overflowing with the charm of country trim. Colonial-syle motifs, a friendly sheep, and a heart of country blue combine with traditional Christmas decorations to bedeck every room of the house. With a blazing Yule log in the fireplace and the smell of cinnamon and molasses drifting from the kitchen, country crafters add a touch of gingham ribbon or patchwork to that special, handmade Christmas project, creating a new generation of collectibles for families to pass along.

Whether it's in a farmhouse set on a snow-covered plain or a California condo with highway views, country expresses the heart of Christmas with a look that says, "Merry Christmas, America."

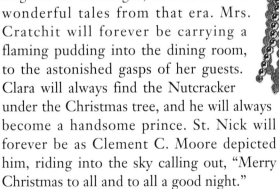

A Victorian Christmas brings to mind carriage wheels rolling along snow-covered streets, shop windows filled with magical toys, and a bounteous banquet spread on a gleaming table. More than any other Yuletide celebration, Victorian Christmas means formality, festivity, and family.

We view the Christmas of long ago through the warm glow of nostalgia, thanks to the wonderful tales from that era. Mrs. Cratchit will forever be carrying a flaming pudding into the dining room, to the astonished gasps of her guests. Clara will always find the Nutcracker under the Christmas tree, and he will always become a handsome prince. St. Nick will forever be as Clement C. Moore depicted him, riding into the sky calling out, "Merry Christmas to all and to all a good night."

Today more than ever before, we seek to capture the feeling this sentimental picture of Christmas past creates. Candlelight and rich foods, dancing flames in a marble fireplace, glass baubles that sparkle from a little fir tree . . . this is the promise of Victorian Christmas.

Torches, candles, and bonfires lit the cold, dark days and nights in Scandinavia long before Christianity and Christmas arrived on its shores. By brightening the long winter, Norsemen tried to keep away the gloom until spring's welcome arrival.

With the advent of Christianity, Christmas celebrations continued these centuries-old traditions as the Feast of Lights. Families gathered together to decorate their winter homes with color and candles, customs and symbols. Christmas became a time to share crafting skills and the best recipes with family and friends, and to set out a sheaf of wheat for the birds.

Today the Feast of Lights continues across America in families of Scandinavian heritage and among those who appreciate the charm of its design. Straw goats, woven ornaments, red satin hearts and Santa Lucia's crown of candles are delightful decorations for any family to enjoy, and one doesn't have to be Scandinavian to savor pancakes filled with lingonberries. Once you become familiar with the simple beauty of a Scandinavian Christmas, traditions from the Feast of Lights can illuminate your Yuletide season.

Luminarias on a tile walkway, chile wreaths, Mexican biscuits—Christmas in the Southwest takes the beauty of ancient Spanish customs and gives them a contemporary twist. The effect is timeless, a blend of sunny desert and snowy mountain, Anglo and Indian, spirit and place. The Southwest is a part of America where the best, most beautiful elements of a region's heritage create a new culture with unique holiday celebrations.

It's a zesty tradition of spicy food, bold colors, and a festive atmosphere. Folk arts from south of the border to the high Sierras nestle under a Christmas tree decorated with ornaments in colors ranging from earthtones to pastels and fashioned from materials as natural as clay and wool. A cactus and greens on the mantel? Why not.

Under the open skies of the Southwest, craftspeople express all the wonders of their region. Let their crafts and customs bring a new sense of joy to your home this Christmas.

Table of Contents

Country Christmas

Show your colors this holiday season

Celebrate America's favorite holiday with America's favorite style.

Greenery and pine, quilt and gingham, bears and flags—these are the down-home delights of America's Christmas, reflecting our rural heritage and colonial design. Nestle your favorite country keepsakes beside a cozy hearth, with a red quilt nearby for extra warmth. Light a candle on the coffee table, and drape evergreen above your door. Add a fife and drum to your tree, or mix stars and stripes with traditional hearts. When you decorate with the comfortable look of old-fashioned Americana, you're keeping the Christmas spirit of our country!

A sun-filled
room awaits the
big day with country
charm: shining
pewter, evergreens,
and treasured
ornaments.

A bevy of bears peeks from behind stair railings,

awaiting the arrival of holiday guests, while a family of

bears plays winter games in the kitchen.

*T*he family cat

takes a winter nap,

dreaming of what his

stocking will hold.

A brigade of cheery nutcrackers gathers to salute a patriotic tree. What youngster wouldn't be enchanted by this Christmas scene?

A light-filled trunk overflows with greenery and gifts, the hallmarks of Christmas. The shimmering tree provides the perfect background for a holiday dinner party.

Victorian Splendor

Elegance and a Touch of Whimsy

A **Victorian Christmas is a romantic vision, like a Currier and Ives print that's come to life.**

Fine furnishings, cherished collectibles, flickering candles . . . and in the center, a courtly Christmas tree. The Victorian home at Christmas glows with rich jewel tones and sumptuous fabrics. On the mantel, above a crackling fire, cherubic angels offer winsome smiles. Silver bells catch the fire's glow. Candles tower above mahogany tables, their flames dancing in gilt mirrors. The anticipation of hoped-for gifts and special visits puts magic in the air. For those who long to live their holidays with grace and ceremony, only the regal pace of Victorian Christmas will do.

*T*he good things

in life look even better

at Christmas when

the world sparkles

and shines.

A quiet corner plays host to a towering Christmas tree. The very walls seem to eagerly anticipate the imminent arrival of guests, while the packages on the loveseat keep their secrets for a few more minutes.

*A*n ancestor of long ago casts an approving eye on Christmas trim. Comforting heirloom decorations placed in familiar locations are traditions that warm our hearts.

*V*oices of past celebrations

echo through these rooms. A

family gathers together to sing

Yuletide songs, and a teapot

awaits a mother's steady hand.

Whut is a Victorian Christmas?

A tree with handmade decorations.

A sumptuous meal on a carefully

arranged table. A ribbon-wrapped tree

that's delicate as a teacup.

Scandinavian Season
Memorable Customs

Delight in an old-world atmosphere brimming with holiday excitement.

In Scandinavia, the sun sets early on Christmas Eve. The earth is hushed, the evening sky is azure blue, and children run excitedly to close shutters and doors. Mother lights the candles, while Father gathers enough firewood to last the night. The home is decorated in age-old style, with happy hues of red and white dominating the scene. Decorations fashioned of wood and straw are lovingly unwrapped and displayed. For a few hours the children's eyes glitter with the light of the jumping hearth fire, and the snow and the wind are distant companions.

*A*fter a day playing outside, it's time to come indoors. There are straw decorations to fashion and cookies to bake. Holiday quilts come out of storage to decorate stair railings and cover soft featherbeds.

*T*he clean lines and bright colors of Scandinavian

Christmas are right at home in a contemporary

setting. Greenery and St. Nick figurines set the tone

in every room.

With the children off to school, present wrapping can begin. The great day is just around the corner, and the tree seems to want packages to keep it company.

*A*ll about the house it's

Christmastime. Wheat, bundled

with bright ribbon, bedecks

each nook and cranny.

*T*raditional Scandina-
vian decorations are
displayed in a pretty
fairyland setting. A Santa
Lucia doll holds court
over a miniature world of
bright straw animals,
hearts, and blue-and-
white china.

Southwest Festivity
Warm and Inviting

A banner of stars twinkles in the desert sky like tiny Christmas lights above the horizon.

Light in all its forms—faint and flickering, bold and subdued—is the hallmark of a Southwest Christmas. Whether a bonfire flickers in a city square or luminarias light the way home, the fires that burn at Christmas warm the heart and soul. Based on ethnic traditions that date back centuries, Southwest Christmas is a truly American celebration. But luminarias, nativity scenes, and chile ristras tell only part of the story. For it is the family, the center of Latin American life, that is the most important element of these holiday settings.

Splendid outdoor vistas are just a step away in the Southwest. This elegant home creates the spacious feeling of a Spanish villa with two interior courtyards.

*E*choing with the sounds of romantic ballads played

on an old guitar, this stucco dining room shimmers with the

desert colors of the Southwest. A table set for a traditional

holiday dinner means that tasty ethnic dishes—chile

rellenos, tamales, and empanaditas— are only minutes away.

Set on a brightly striped tablecloth, the colorful centerpiece

is surrounded by kachina-style dolls.

A barnyard of handcrafted animals, painted and carved, gathers in a holiday dining room. Wonderful and whimsical, they typify the Southwest Christmas.

*F*ront doors offer a Southwest salute to passing friends and family at Christmastime. The wreaths and lights seem to say, "Stop and enjoy a cup of Christmas cheer."

*W*hen Southwest-
erners say, "I'll be home
for Christmas," they
probably imagine a set-
ting like this, with lum-
inarias, equipal chairs,
and tin ornaments.

Christmas Table

A Banquet of Memories and Mirth

Food, family, and friends provide the recipe for holiday happiness.

Think of Christmas and you think of gingerbread cookies on a frosty afternoon, creamy eggnog before the fire, and a formal Christmas dinner table surrounded by family members young and old. At no other time of year is food more important and symbolic than during the holidays. Our most treasured Christmas memories and our fondest hopes for Christmases yet to come include images of flour-dusted hands, bent and battered recipe cards, and bewitching aromas drifting from the kitchen. Come raise a glass to the bounty of the Christmas table!

COUNTRY CAROLING POTLUCK
A Supper to Sing About

Festive and flavorful, this yuletide buffet chases away winter's chill.

Angel Biscuits with Ham Slices

Hidden Valley Ranch Crunchy Pea Salad

Sauerkraut Relish

Blueberry Cream Cake

Sing 'n' Sip Cider

The last chorus of "Silent Night" fades into the crisp, snowy air, and at last it's time to head for home. Tweaked by the nippy night cold, our cheeks are ruddy and our toes tingle, but spirits soar. An evening of strolling through the snow, voices raised clear and strong, kindles a powerful appetite.

This cheery country buffet serves up old favorites with a new twist. It's home-style cooking at its best. Even after the last crumb is eaten and the bottom-of-the-barrel puddle of cider is all that's left, your guests will still feel like singing.

Angel Biscuits with Ham Slices

1 package active dry yeast
2 cups buttermilk (divided)
5 cups all-purpose flour
¼ cup sugar
1 tablespoon baking powder
1 teaspoon salt
1 teaspoon baking soda
1 cup vegetable shortening
Melted butter
Thin slices of ham, if desired

Mix yeast with ¼ cup of the buttermilk; set aside. Stir together flour, sugar, baking powder, salt and baking soda; cut in shortening. Add yeast mixture and remaining buttermilk and mix well. (Dough will be slightly sticky.)

Place in refrigerator, covered, until ready to use. Scoop out needed amount and roll on floured surface to ⅜-inch thickness and cut into biscuits about 2 inches in diameter.

Place cut biscuits onto baking sheet; brush lightly with melted butter and place another biscuit on top, brushing tops with butter.

Bake at 400° for 10-12 minutes or until lightly browned on top. To serve, separate biscuits and place thin ham slice between layers, if desired. Yield: 24 biscuits.

Hidden Valley Ranch Crunchy Pea Salad

1 package (10 ounces) frozen peas, thawed, dried on paper towel
1 cup diced celery
1 cup chopped cauliflower
¼ cup thinly sliced green onions
½ cup dairy sour cream
1 cup Hidden Valley Ranch dressing
1 cup cashews, broken
4 strips lean center cut bacon, fried, drained, crumbled

In a medium size mixing bowl, combine peas, celery, cauliflower, and green onions. In a separate small bowl, whisk together sour cream and Ranch dressing. Spoon 1 cup of dressing over salad ingredients, fold together gently. Add additional dressing, if desired. Cover; chill.

Before serving, stir in cashews and garnish with crumbled bacon. Yield: 6-8 servings.

Sauerkraut Relish

1 large package fresh sauerkraut, drained
1 cup granulated sugar
1 cup cider vinegar
1 cup chopped onion
1 jar (2 ounces) diced pimiento
½ cup chopped green pepper

Place sauerkraut in large bowl; set aside. Combine sugar and vinegar with whisk, mixing until sugar begins to dissolve. Stir in onion, pimiento, and pepper. Add to sauerkraut, mixing to blend. Put into glass two-quart container with lid. Refrigerate for at least three days before eating. Yield: 10-12 servings.

Blueberry Cream Cake

1 cup granulated sugar
½ cup margarine, room temperature
2 large eggs, room temperature
1 teaspoon vanilla
2 cups all-purpose flour
1½ teaspoons baking powder
1 teaspoon baking soda
¼ teaspoon salt
1 cup dairy sour cream
1½ cups fresh or frozen blueberries, rinsed and dried
1¼ cups shredded coconut
1½ cups heavy whipping cream, whipped
Large fresh blueberries for garnish
Granulated sugar for garnish

In a large mixing bowl, beat together the 1 cup sugar, margarine, eggs, and vanilla until light and lemon colored. Sift together flour, baking powder, soda, and salt. Beat into creamed mixture alternately with sour cream. Beat until light and fluffy. Gently fold in berries with a rubber spatula, being careful not to break berries.

Spoon batter into two well-greased 9-inch layer cake pans. Sprinkle top of batter with coconut; bake at 350° for about 30-35 minutes or until wooden toothpick comes out clean. Remove from oven. Cool on wire racks for 5 minutes.

Place waxed paper over pans; invert cakes onto wire racks, then invert again so coconut is right side up. Remove papers; cool thoroughly. Just before serving put cake layers together with whipped cream. Garnish top with whipped cream and large berries dipped in granulated sugar. Refrigerate any leftovers. Yield: 10-12 servings.

Sing 'n' Sip Cider

2 quarts fresh unpasturized apple cider
1 tablespoon lemon juice
2 tablespoons brown sugar
4 cinnamon sticks
1 teaspoon whole cloves
1 teaspoon whole allspice berries
1 cup Calvados or applejack

Dissolve brown sugar in cider in large saucepan. Add lemon juice and heat to boiling. Wrap spices in cheesecloth bag, or use large spice ball. When cider comes to boil, add spices and let steep for 15-20 minutes.

In separate pan, heat applejack gently until just warm. Add to cider mixture and serve piping hot in warm mugs. Yield: 8 cups.

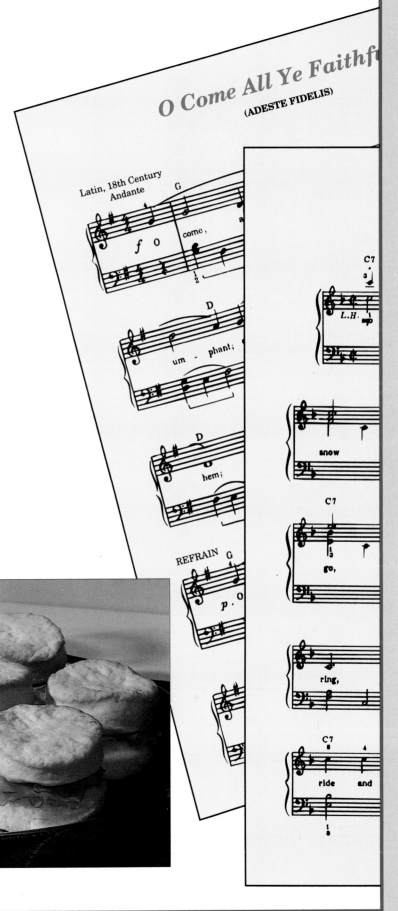

VICTORIAN
FARE
A Warming Feast

Fine china and friends will make this dinner an occasion to remember.

Victorian Mustard Soup
Hearty Winter Pie
Sherry-Glazed Onions
Frothy Eggnog Pudding

Our Victorian dinner, inspired by an after-the-hunt feast, will be a welcome sight (and smell) for hungry guests coming in from the cold. We planned our dinner to be reminiscent of Old World dishes while using the finest American ingredients. Hearty and traditional, this dinner is sure to become a Christmas classic that friends and family will happily anticipate every holiday season. While the wind roars outside, this delicious fare will have you shouting, "Tally-ho!"

Victorian Mustard Soup

2 tablespoons unsalted butter
2 medium-size onions, thinly sliced
¾ lb. mushrooms, sliced
2 cups cream
3 cups milk
3 tablespoons Dijon mustard
¼ teaspoon tarragon
Salt and pepper
Fresh parsley, chopped

Melt butter in large saucepan and add onions. Cook for about three minutes or until onions are soft but not brown. Add the mushrooms and tarragon and cook over low heat for three minutes. Add the cream, milk, and mustard. Heat gently, but do not allow the soup to boil.

Season to taste with salt and pepper; garnish with fresh parsley and serve immediately. Yield: 6 servings.

Hearty Winter Pie

3 tablespoons butter
3 tablespoons chopped shallots
½ cup thinly sliced mushrooms
3 tablespoons flour
Dash tarragon
Dash pepper
2 cups beef stock
1 tablespoon Worcestershire sauce
1 tablespoon chopped parsley
1 garlic clove, minced
1 bay leaf
2 cups round steak cubes, cooked
Carrots
1 cup port wine
Pie crust (recipe below)

Melt butter in frying pan. Stir in shallots and mushrooms. Cook for 4 minutes, stirring constantly. Sprinkle with flour, tarragon, and pepper. Add beef stock and cook slowly, stirring constantly until mixture boils and thickens. Add Worcestershire sauce, chopped parsley, garlic, bay leaf, beef cubes, and carrots. Cook for 3 minutes, then discard bay leaf.

Turn into deep pie dish. Cover with pie crust. Press edges firmly and vent top of crust. Bake at 400° for 12 to 15 minutes or until crust is brown. Place a small funnel in one of the vents and pour port wine into the pie. Bake for 2 to 3 minutes longer and serve. Yield: 6-8 servings.

Pie Crust

1½ cups flour
¼ teaspoon salt
½ cup shortening
3-4 tablespoons cold water

Mix flour and salt. Cut in shortening with pastry blender. Blend until mixture resembles coarse meal. Slowly sprinkle water over flour mixture and mix with fork until dough forms a ball. Roll dough 2 inches larger than pan and proceed as above.

Sherry-Glazed Onions

4 tablespoons butter
1½ lbs. pearl onions
¾ cup chicken stock
3 tablespoons cream sherry
2 tablespoons sugar
3 tablespoons bread crumbs

Melt 1½ tablespoons butter in sauce pan. Add onions and stir to coat well. Add chicken stock, sherry, and sugar; simmer until onions are tender. Drizzle melted butter and bread crumbs over onions. Simmer an additional 2 to 3 minutes or until liquid is completely absorbed and serve. Yield: 6-8 servings.

Frothy Eggnog Pudding

4 cups eggnog
3 tablespoons cornstarch
4 tablespoons milk
1 teaspoon salt
4 tablespoons rum
4 cups cooked rice
Whipped cream
Nutmeg

Victorian Dinner

Too often, the china we receive as wedding gifts goes unused. It sits in a hutch rather than on a dinner table. This Christmas, why not use those elegant plates and cups? It's a way of telling guests, "Only the best will do for you. This meal will tempt both your palate and your eyes."

Heat eggnog over low heat. Combine cornstarch and milk. Pour into eggnog, stirring constantly. Cook and stir over low heat until mixture thickens. Add salt and rum. Fold in cooked rice. Pour into individual dishes; chill. Serve with whipped cream and a sprinkle of nutmeg. Yield: 8 servings.

SCANDINAVIAN BREAKFAST
Delightful treats to start your Christmas Day

Fresh-tasting herbs, sweet fruits, and rich breads create a perfect morning meal.

Nordic Egg Skillet

Scandinavian Fruit Soup

Astrid's Pancakes with Lingonberries

Swedish Cardamom Coffeecake

What better time to sample holiday food from the far north than on Christmas Day! Thanks to our Scandinavian immigrants who brought us their best holiday recipes packed in their steamer trunks, we can enjoy a sublime breakfast such as this. While everyone's admiring those new gifts, brew another pot of coffee and sample the dark taste of braided cardamom coffee cake. Then sit down to a refreshing bowl of fruit soup, eggs accented with dill, and Sweden's snowflake-thin pancakes with tangy lingonberries. Here's a delicious heritage of cool flavors and bright colors that will wish your family a Merry Christmas the Scandinavian way.

Nordic Egg Skillet

6 eggs
3 tablespoons condensed milk
1 teaspoon salt
Dash of pepper
2 dill pickles, sliced or diced
2 tablespoons chives
2 tablespoons chopped dill
8 ounces Danish cheese, diced
3 tablespoons butter
2 tomatoes
1 extra tablespoon chives (for garnish)

Mix eggs with milk, salt, and pepper in bowl. Add pickles, chives, dill, and cheese. Heat butter in large skillet and add egg mixture. Cover, simmering on low heat 10 minutes.

While eggs are cooking, wash, peel, and quarter tomatoes. When egg mixture has set in middle, place tomatoes on top for decoration and sprinkle with chives. Serve at once. Yield: 6-8 servings.

Scandinavian Fruit Soup

¼ pound dried prunes
¼ pound dried apricots
¼ pound dried apples
¼ pound raisins
1 quart water
1 cinnamon stick
1 16-oz. can cherries, drained
½ cup sugar
Juice of half lemon
Rind of half lemon, grated
½ cup tapioca

Soak dried fruits in cold water for 2 to 3 hours. Cook slowly in same water with cinnamon stick until fruit is tender. Add cherries and sugar, lemon juice and rind, and tapioca. Cook until slightly thick. Cool and serve.

Astrid's Pancakes with Lingonberries

4 eggs
2 cups milk
1½ cups flour
2 teaspoons sugar
Dash salt
Butter
1 jar lingonberries
Powdered sugar

Beat eggs, then add milk. Gradually add flour. While stirring, add sugar and salt, then beat until batter is smooth and thin.

Melt butter in a non-stick pan and pour batter in two teaspoonsful at a time to make 6-inch pancakes. When bubbles form around edge of pancake, flip over. When pancake is firm and dry, remove from pan. Repeat until no batter remains.

To serve: Place approximately 2 tablespoons of lingonberries down the center of pancake. Flip edges of pancake into center, as you would for a crepe. Place on plate with edges underneath and cut three diagonal slices in rolled pancake. Sprinkle with powdered sugar and serve immediately. Yield: 8 pancakes.

Swedish Cardamom Coffeecake

1¼ cups milk
1 package active dry yeast
¼ cup lukewarm water (100°-105°)
1 tablespoon sugar
6 cups sifted all-purpose flour, divided
¾ cup sugar
½ cup butter, softened
3 egg yolks
1 tablespoon ground cardamom
¾ teaspoon salt
¼ cup chopped walnuts
2 tablespoons sugar
2 teaspoons cinnamon
Milk

In a saucepan, heat 1¼ cups milk to lukewarm (100°-105°). Set aside. In a bowl, combine yeast and ¼ cup lukewarm water with 1 tablespoon sugar to proof yeast. (Small bubbles will form on surface ensuring yeast's leavening abilities.) Combine yeast mixture with milk and beat in 3 cups of flour.

Cover; let rise in a warm place for 1½ hours. Beat in 2¾ cups flour, ¾ cup sugar, softened butter, egg yolks, cardamom and salt.

Turn dough onto lightly floured surface. Knead in remaining ¼ cup flour or enough to make smooth dough, kneading for 15 minutes. Place dough in lightly greased bowl; turn once to grease surface. Cover; let rise in a warm place until double (about 1 hour).

Divide dough into 6 equal portions. On lightly floured surface, roll each piece into a rope 16 inches long on a greased baking sheet. Pinch the ends of three ropes together. Braid the ropes loosely and pinch the other ends together. Tuck pinched ends under braid. Repeat, braiding remaining 3 ropes of dough in same manner.

Cover and let rise in a warm place until almost double, about 30 minutes.

In a small bowl, combine chopped walnuts, 2 tablespoons sugar, and cinnamon. Brush braids with a little milk, sprinkle tops with cinnamon mixture. Bake at 375° about 25 minutes or until golden brown. Cool on wire racks. Yield: 2 coffeecakes.

NORWEGIAN
Wreath Cake

For a truly traditional holiday centerpiece, many Scandinavians make a Norwegian Wreath Cake like the one pictured on page 69. This cake adds an authentically Nordic look to any special occasion, such as weddings, confirmations, and of course Christmas.

Eighteen wreaths are made from a moist, chewy almond batter that is rolled into ropes and baked in special *kransekake* molds or, if these special pans are unavailable, shaped by hand. Each wreath is a slightly different diameter, ranging from 2 to 10 inches wide, so that they can be stacked into a tapered tower. Sugar or toothpicks glue the rings together, and some people slip the rings over a tall, thin wine bottle for extra support. Icing, small flags, or paper party snappers add the finishing decorative touch. After the meal is over, the wreaths can be enjoyed to the last crumb — sweet souvenirs of a memorable celebration.

SOUTHWEST
CHRISTMAS
DINNER
A Piquant Feast

You don't have to live in the Southwest to love hot and spicy turkey.

Chile-Rubbed Turkey with Pumpkin Seed Sauce and Double Cornbread Stuffing

Squash Salpicon

Jicama, Avocado, and Mango Salad

Pumpkin Pine Nut Tart

Gathering around the traditional Christmas turkey with family and friends takes on an authentic American flavor when foods are seasoned Southwest style. Tempt the taste buds with regional variations that showcase Southwestern cuisine in the rich use of corn, coriander, squash, peppers, pine nuts and pumpkin seeds. Chiles, rubbed into the turkey, double cornbread stuffing with chorizo and fresh coriander, and pumpkin seed sauce perfectly complement the turkey. Now this is Christmas dinner with a difference!

Chile-Rubbed Turkey with Pumpkin Seed Sauce and Double Cornbread Stuffing

Double Cornbread Stuffing
1 cup yellow cornmeal
1 teaspoon baking powder
½ teaspoon baking soda
½ teaspoon salt
¼ teaspoon cayenne pepper
1 cup corn kernels
1 cup cultured sour cream
1 can (4 ounces) diced chiles, undrained
4 ounces grated Monterey Jack cheese
   (about 1 cup)
4 tablespoons unsalted butter
1 pound chorizo, casing removed,
   cut into ¼-inch slices, halved
⅓ cup chopped fresh coriander

Chile Sauce
¼ cup orange juice
2 tablespoons Oriental chile paste with garlic
2 tablespoons distilled white vinegar
2 tablespoons finely chopped fresh coriander
2 tablespoons blanched, diced orange peel
1 teaspoon ground cinnamon
1 teaspoon salt
½ teaspoon freshly ground pepper
1 fresh turkey (14 pounds)
½ cup unsalted butter, melted

Pumpkin Seed Sauce
1 pound fresh or canned tomatillos
4 ounces toasted, hulled, unsalted
   pumpkin seeds
½ cup chopped onion
2 jalapeño peppers, seeded, diced
2 cloves garlic, chopped
½ teaspoon sugar
½ teaspoon salt
½ teaspoon freshly ground pepper
1½ cups chicken broth or more as needed

Heat oven to 400°. Grease 9-inch square pan or well-seasoned cast iron skillet. In large bowl, combine cornmeal, baking powder, baking soda, salt, and cayenne pepper. Add corn kernels, sour cream, chiles, cheese, and butter, stirring until blended. Pour into prepared pan; bake until golden brown, 25-30 minutes. Let cool completely.

Meanwhile, in large skillet, cook chorizo over medium heat, stirring constantly until browned, 8-10 minutes. Drain on paper towels. In large bowl, crumble cornbread; stir in chorizo and coriander. Yield: 6 cups.

To make chile sauce, combine orange juice, chile paste, vinegar, coriander, orange peel, cinnamon, salt, and pepper in small bowl, stirring to blend. Set aside.

To prepare turkey, heat oven to 350°. Rinse turkey inside and out; pat dry with paper towels. Sprinkle turkey inside and outside with salt and pepper to taste. Stuff body and neck cavities loosely with stuffing; close both ends with trussing skewers and string.

Fold wings under and push wing tips firmly under back. Place turkey, breast side up, on rack in roasting pan. Brush melted butter directly over skin. Pour chile sauce over turkey, brushing lightly to cover surface. Cover with roasting pan cover or aluminum foil tent. Roast turkey in oven about 15-18 minutes per pound, basting with pan juice every 30 minutes. After 3½ hours, remove cover and continue to roast about 45 minutes until meat thermometer inserted in thickest part of thigh registers 170° to 175°. Transfer turkey to cutting board or large platter. Let stand 20-30 minutes before carving, while making pumpkin seed sauce. Yield: 20-28 servings.

To make pumpkin seed sauce, heat broiler. Place tomatillos on baking pan with sides; broil 4 inches from heat, turning until skin is dark and blistered on all sides, 8-10 minutes. Place in bowl with any juices; cool completely. (If using canned tomatillos, just drain and place in food processor.)

Meanwhile, place pumpkin seeds in food processor; process until finely ground. Peel skin from tomatillos and discard. Place tomatillos in food processor with any juices that accumulate. Add onion, jalapeño pepper, garlic, sugar, salt, and pepper; process until blended. Pour sauce into large skillet; heat over medium heat until hot. Add chicken broth as needed to thin to a sauce consistency. Yield: 4 cups.

Squash Salpicon

2 tablespoons unsalted butter
1½ cups finely chopped onion

1 each small red, green, yellow bell pepper,
    seeded, cut into ½-inch dice
2 jalapeño peppers, seeded, diced
2 cloves garlic, minced
½ pound butternut or Hubbard squash,
    pared, cut into ½-inch dice
½ pound zucchini, trimmed, cut into ½-
    inch dice
1 cup corn kernels
1 teaspoon salt
½ teaspoon dried oregano
¼ teaspoon freshly ground pepper
3 tablespoons heavy cream
4 ounces Monterey Jack cheese,
    finely grated

In 9- or 10-inch ovenproof skillet, melt butter over medium heat. Add onion, bell peppers, jalapeño pepper, and garlic; cook, stirring frequently until softened, 5-7 minutes. Add squash, zucchini, corn, salt, oregano, and pepper. Cook, covered, stirring occasionally, 7-8 minutes. Heat broiler.

Pour cream around sides of skillet and cook, uncovered, until vegetables just begin to lightly brown, about 5-7 minutes. Sprinkle top with cheese; broil 4 inches from heat until cheese is melted and browned, 1-2 minutes. Yield: 6 cups.

Jicama, Avocado, and Mango Salad

2 heads Boston lettuce, rinsed, dried
1 bunch watercress, stems removed
½ pound jicama, pared, cut into julienne
    cuts (about 2 cups), optional
2 pink grapefruits, pared, white pith
    removed, cut into segments, juice
    reserved (about ⅓ cup)
2 mangos pared, cut into ¼-inch slices
2 avocados, pared, pitted, cut into
    1¼-inch slices
1 red onion, thinly sliced
Vinaigrette dressing

In large salad bowl arrange lettuce leaves, watercress, jicama, grapefruit, mango, avocado and onion. Drizzle dressing over salad just before serving. Yield: 12 servings.

Pumpkin Pine Nut Tart

Pastry Crust:
½ cup toasted pine nuts
1¼ cups all-purpose flour
3 tablespoons dark brown sugar (packed)
½ teaspoon cinnamon
½ cup unsalted butter, cold,
    cut into small pieces
1 teaspoon vanilla

Filling:
3 cups plain canned pumpkin
¾ cup dark brown sugar (packed)
3 large eggs, beaten
½ cup heavy cream
2 teaspoons vanilla
1 teaspoon ground cinnamon
½ teaspoon ground clove
½ teaspoon ground ginger
½ teaspoon ground nutmeg

Topping:
6 tablespoons all-purpose flour
¼ cup dark brown sugar (packed)
4 tablespoons unsalted butter,
    at room temperature
¾ cup toasted pine nuts

Heat oven to 425°. Process pine nuts and flour in food processor until chopped. Add sugar and cinnamon, butter and vanilla; process until mixture begins to form a ball. Press pastry over bottom and up side of 10-10½-inch tart pan with removable bottom. Refrigerate until ready to bake.

To prepare filling, whisk pumpkin, sugar, eggs, heavy cream, vanilla, cinnamon, clove, ginger, and nutmeg in large bowl until well blended. Place tart on baking sheet and pour filling into crust. Bake tart 20 minutes. Reduce heat to 350°; bake 20 minutes longer.

Meanwhile, prepare topping. In small bowl, combine flour and sugar. Add butter; work into sugar mixture with fork or pastry blender until blended. Stir in pine nuts.

Sprinkle topping evenly over surface of tart. Return to oven; bake until topping is crisp, 8-10 minutes, and custard tests done with knife. Cool completely on wire rack. Serve with unsweetened whipped cream or vanilla ice cream, if desired. Yield: 12 servings.

STARS & BARS

Family and friends will salute these Christmas treats.

Cookies with coast-to-coast flavor display America's holiday spirit.

Santa Fe Chocolate Stars

1½ oz. Mexican chocolate
(Mexican chocolate consists of chocolate, cinnamon, and sugar. It comes in tablets or bars. Look for it in the ethnic foods section of your grocery store.)
½ cup butter, room temperature
¼ cup sugar
3 tablespoons honey
½ teaspoon almond extract
1 egg
2 cups all-purpose flour
⅛ teaspoon salt
Sliced almonds, chocolate chips, and chocolate sprinkles for decoration

Place chocolate in small bowl and melt in microwave. Combine softened chocolate and butter in large bowl and beat until smooth. Add the sugar and honey, beating until mixture is fluffy. Add almond extract and egg; blend. Stir in flour and salt. Form dough into a ball, cover with plastic wrap and chill for 3 to 4 hours or overnight. Preheat oven to 350°. Roll out dough ¼-inch thick and cut with star-shaped cookie cutters. Decorate cookies with slices of almond, chocolate chips, or chocolate sprinkles. Bake for 12 to 15 minutes on ungreased cookie sheets. Cool on rack. Makes 30 (2-inch) stars.

New England Apple Bars

1½ cups dried apples, chopped
1½ cups all-purpose flour
½ teaspoon baking soda
½ teaspoon cinnamon
¼ teaspoon nutmeg
¼ teaspoon salt
½ cup butter or margarine
¾ cup packed brown sugar
2 eggs
½ cup apple butter
½ cup chopped walnuts

Pour enough boiling water over apple bits to cover, then let stand 5 minutes. Drain. Meanwhile, stir together flour, baking soda, spices, and salt. In a large mixing bowl beat butter or margarine until softened. Add brown sugar and beat until fluffy. Add eggs and apple butter and continue to beat well. Add flour mixture, combining thoroughly.

Stir in drained fruit and nuts. Spread in greased 13x9x2-inch baking pan. Bake in a 350° oven for 25 to 30 minutes or until done. Cool. Sift powdered sugar over cookies and cut into bars. Makes 36.

Heartland Spice Stars

**3 cups sifted
  all-purpose flour**
**2 teaspoons ground
  cinnamon**
**2 teaspoons
  ground ginger**
½ teaspoon ground cloves
**⅜ cup plus 2 tablespoons
  butter or margarine**
1½ cups sugar
1 egg
4 tablespoons honey
2 teaspoons soda
1 tablespoon warm water
**Grated rind of
  large orange**

Sift together flour, salt, and spices. Cream butter; add sugar and continue to cream. Beat in egg and honey. Dissolve soda in warm water and add to creamed mixture. Add orange rind and sifted dry ingredients. Mix well, adding 1 to 2 tablespoons water if necessary to form firm dough. Chill several hours or overnight. Roll out ⅛-inch thick and cut into star shapes. Bake on ungreased cookie sheets at 400° for 5 to 10 minutes. Cool. Frost with thin icing made from 1 cup sifted powdered sugar and 1 tablespoon milk. Makes 50 cookies.

Beacon Hill Raspberry Bars

For base:
1 cup flour
1 teaspoon baking powder
½ cup butter, softened
1 egg
1 tablespoon milk
½ cup raspberry jam

For topping:
1 egg
⅔ cup sugar
¼ cup butter, melted
1 teaspoon vanilla extract

Preheat oven to 450°. For base, combine flour and baking powder in a large bowl. Cut in butter with hand mixer or pastry blender until mixture resembles cornmeal. Stir in egg and milk to form soft dough. Press dough into bottom of ungreased 9x9-inch pan. Spread jam evenly over dough. For topping, stir egg, sugar, butter, and vanilla in small bowl. Carefully spread on top of jam. Bake at 350° for 35 to 40 minutes or until browned. Cool on rack, then cut into bars. Makes 24 bars.

Christmas Crafts

Handmade from the Heart

Share your talents by making these easy holiday projects to keep or give as presents.

With needle and thread, paint and brush, glitter and glue, Americans revel in the giving season. Whether it's a quilt painstakingly pieced by hand or a simple paper snowflake, handcrafts satisfy our desire to give something of ourselves to others. See how the colors of Old Glory can add a patriotic look to a holiday centerpiece. Add a nosegay ornament to a collection of Christmas tree heirlooms, or braid a wheat wreath to brighten a winter window. Paint a trinket box and fill it with potpourri, then personalize your gift with one-of-a-kind hand-painted wrapping paper. Americans love making special Christmas treasures and giving these prizes to those they love.

The Art of Country

An American heritage of creativity

Country crafters relish the Christmas season.

Before the frost is on the pumpkin, a crafter begins planning for Christmas. Finding clever uses for fabric scraps, dried foliage, or bits of ribbon is a challenge, one that inspires pretty—and practical—gifts. Wood, wool, and berries—you'll love adding these materials to fashion a special something for that special someone. Because of their simple designs, country crafts can be surprisingly contemporary while echoing our colonial traditions. The spirit of American Christmas thrives in the crafter's workshop.

Quilted Stocking

Materials:
Old quilt square, 9" square
Muslin, 9" x 12"
Red flannel for lining, 9" x 12"
Ribbon, 1⅛" wide, 4 inches
Fleece, 2 pieces, 9" x 6"
Matching sewing thread

Directions:
1. Cut one boot shape from quilt square, one from muslin, 2 from fleece, and 2 from lining.
2. Baste one piece of fleece to back of quilt boot and one to muslin. Place lining on right side of quilt boot and sew across top. Place second piece of lining on right side of muslin boot and sew across top. Open both boot-pairs flat. Press seams towards lining.
3. Place quilt/lining piece on top of muslin/lining piece with extended lining sections together. Starting at back near top of cuff, sew around entire outer edge, leaving a 2½" opening for turning. Trim, clip seams, and turn.
4. Fold ribbon in half and attach ends 1½" from top seam on lining side. Slip-stitch opening shut.
5. Push lining down inside stocking and push toe into outer stocking. Iron if necessary to flatten seams. Fold cuff over 1 inch to show inner lining.

Cut
1 Quilt Square
1 Muslin
2 Fleece
2 Lining

Use photocopy machine to enlarge pattern 200%.

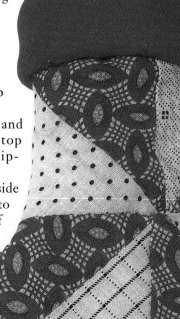

Materials:

Assorted rag stockings

Red sewing thread

For Western Stocking: bandana and
  Western-style charms or buttons

For Rickrack Stocking: jumbo rickrack, large
  enameled jingle bells, 1 yard red and 1½
  yards green rayon cording and craft glue

For Ruffled Stocking: red and black plaid
  wool fabric, approximately 5" x 60"

For Cuffed Stocking: cuff with buttons from
  man's plaid shirt, plus a scrap of shirt's fabric approximately 4" x 7"

Directions:

Western Stocking

1. Fold bandana in half diagonally. Wrap loosely around top of sock as shown in photo.
2. Pin in place, stretching sock slightly.
3. Tie bandana.
4. Slipstitch to top of sock. Sew on charms or buttons as desired.

Rickrack Stocking

1. Glue rickrack to sock as shown, folding cut ends under to keep them from raveling.

2. Cut two 12" long pieces of green cording and one of red cording.
3. Thread a jingle bell onto each and fold cording in half to make loops.
4. Position the cut ends of the loops at the top of the sock, over the rickrack.
5. Cut one 24" length of red cording and one of green. Hold them together and tie into bow.
6. Place the knot of the bow over the cut ends of the loops. Adjust lengths as desired.
7. Sew loops and bow to top of sock. Sew two jingle bells over knot of bow.

Ruffled Stocking

1. Fold wool strip in half with long edges together.
2. Treating them as one layer, gather long edges, adjusting ruffle to fit loosely around top of sock and down back as shown.
3. Pin in place with raw edge to back of sock and inside of top.
4. Stitch ruffle to sock along gathering line.

Cuffed Stocking

1. Turn down top of sock as shown.
2. Place buttoned cuff over it. Fold scrap of fabric over heel of sock, folding in a dart if necessary.
3. Fold under raw edges. Slipstitch both in place.

Papier Maché Country

Materials:

1 bag pre-mixed instant papier maché (can be purchased at most art supply stores)

Acrylic stencil paints. *Colors:* Accent Colors® Acrylic Paints in Sonja Red and Fingerberry Red; Apple Barrel Colors® in Apple Maroon; or mix of these or similar colors

Twigs
(purchased, or find some in your backyard)

Nylon fishing line or upholstery thread

Needle

Hot glue and glue gun

Directions:

1. Follow directions on bag to make papier maché.
2. Roll out dough into balls the size of cranberries, and/or small berries and/or crabapples or larger apples.
3. Spread on waxed paper to dry. While still soft, insert broken twig about 1½" long into apples so it can dry in apple as stem.
4. When berries are dry, paint with small brush and let dry. Apply second coat if needed.
5. For cranberry string, thread needle with nylon fishing line or strong upholstery thread, knot string, and push through cranberries to form string. Form knot around last berry on each end to lock berries.
6. For branch and berry arrangement, heat glue gun. Put drop of hot glue on one berry at a time and stick it to a branch. Cluster 2-3 berries sporadically on branches.
7. Arrange in crock, or insert into grapevine or evergreen wreath for color.

Patriotic Centerpiece

Materials:
- Brass horn
- Green Styrofoam® block, 4" x 9" x 3"
- Felt, 4" x 9", for bottom of block
- Silk greens, 20 picks or equivalent cut from stems
- Silk holly, loose leaves cut from spray
- Dried statice
- Artificial apples, ¾" diameter
- Cinnamon sticks
- Raffia, 6 strands
- Florist's wire, 18 gauge
- American flags on sticks, 4 (may be tea-dyed for antique look)
- Hot glue

Directions:
1. Coil raffia into a loop around hand and tie to hold shape. Wet. Allow to dry. This will make it easier to drape on the arrangement.
2. Glue felt to bottom of Styrofoam block. Wire horn to top of Styrofoam block.
3. Fill base with silk greens.
4. Glue crossed flags in place and drape as desired.
5. Fill greens with dried statice, apples, cinnamon, and holly leaves.
6. Drape raffia as desired and glue in place.

Uncle Sam Santa and Flag-Waving Table Runner

Patriotic Wooden Santa

Materials:

Pine, 9" x 3½" x 2" for Santa and 2¼" x
  3½" x 1½" for stand

Pre-cut wooden star, ¾"

Sandpaper, coarse and fine

Acrylic paint, white, ivory, red, blue, black, pink,
  and gold

White opaque paint pen, if desired

Matte spray finish
Glue

Directions:
1. Trace outline onto wood. Cut shape. Sand all edges of Santa and stand with coarse sandpaper to give a soft, worn look.
2. Transfer details onto cutout. Using photo as a color guide, paint large light areas and then large dark areas. Detail coat with a very fine paint brush or a white opaque paint pen. Paint edges to match front and continue clothing design on back.
3. Paint pre-cut star gold. Glue in place.
4. Paint stand blue. Sand edges of stand lightly. Glue Santa onto stand. Center and

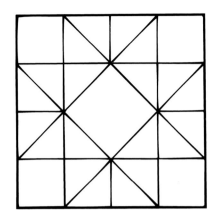

Star Quilt Block diagram

Pattern A

paint white star on front of stand.
5. Apply two light coats of matte spray finish.

Table Runner
Finished size 15½" x 44½"

Materials:
Cotton fabric, 45" wide

Red, 1 yard

Paisley, ½ yard (allow extra if directional pattern)

Ivory with tiny stars, ¼ yard

Ivory, ¼ yard

Navy, ¼ yard

Plaid, ⅛ yard

Cotton quilt batting, 18" x 45"

Matching sewing threads

Invisible sewing thread

Directions:
1. Cut fabric as follows. Dimensions include a ¼" seam allowance on all sides.

Navy triangles from pattern A, 24

Ivory triangles from pattern A, 16

Plaid 3" square, 8

Paisley 4" square, 2

Red band for around block, 1" x 12", 6

Red stripes for center, 1¼" x 20½", 5; and
    2" x 20½", 2 for top and bottom stripes

Paisley for outside bands, 5" x 19", 2; and
    5" x 42", 2

2. Assemble navy and ivory triangles to form 16 squares. Sew one navy triangle to each side of paisley squares. Assemble the 2 star quilt blocks according to the diagram. Sew a 1" x 12" band to three sides of each quilt block. Cut off any excess fabric.

3. Assemble the center striped section with the two larger red bands at the top and bottom. Sew one star quilt block to each end of the striped section.

4. Sew paisley bands to the edges of the runner. Press under ¼" on outer edge.

5. Cut red fabric for backing and cotton quilt batting to size. Baste together backing, batting and pieced table runner. Quilt, as desired. Fold edges of paisley fabric to back of runner leaving a 2¼" finished band around quilt. Slipstitch paisley to backing.

Use photocopy machine to enlarge pattern 200%

Whimsical Wood Nativity

Materials:

Wood
2" x 4" stud, 36" long
2" x 6" joist, 30" long
1" x 3" stock, 4" long for each sheep

Paper-clay, air drying clay available at craft stores

Acrylic paint: white, black, ivory, taupe, brown, tan, rust, maroon, lt. pink, lt. blue, navy blue, teal blue, yellow, metallic gold, metallic purple

Wool roving, "Curly," in white, blond, gray, black, and dark brown

White craft glue and hot glue

Spray finish

Permanent marking pen, extra fine point

Wood stain, Puritan Pine by Minwax

Chenille stems, brown, 2

Synthetic wool, Sherpa, 5" x 7" piece for each sheep

Black felt, 1" square for each sheep

Suede lacing, ⅛" wide, 1 yard

Cotton fabric scraps, embroidery threads, excelsior and batting

Directions:
1. Enlarge patterns and cut figures from wood.
2. Stain manger and camels with wood stain.
3. Roll paper-clay to ¼" thickness. Trace patterns for arms onto paper-clay and cut out with sharp knife. Wet wood where arms will be placed. Lift each arm, gently shape it, smooth edges and press in place on wood. Allow figures to dry overnight.
4. Using photograph as guide, paint figures. Paint areas to be covered by roving a color close to color of roving. Allow to dry. Spray figures with clear finish. Allow to dry.
5. Glue hair and beards in place with craft glue.
6. Draw facial features with permanent marking pen.
7. Drape cloth on heads and manger. Glue in place with craft glue. For Wiseman with cape cut a 6" x 4" piece of fabric. Press all sides under ¼". Run a gathering stitch with gold metallic embroidery thread along one long side. Pull up gathers to fit around neck and tie onto Wiseman.
8. Tie suede lacing around heads of camels for halters. Glue excelsior onto manger. Bend one end of chenille stems into crook and glue to shepherds. Add touches of thread and other trims as desired.
9. Wrap body of sheep with scrap of batting and glue in place. Fold one 7" edge of Sherpa under ½"and glue around neck of sheep. Wrap remainder of Sherpa around sheep, folding under to expose legs as necessary. If using craft glue, hold Sherpa in place with rubberbands and straight pins until glue is dry. Fold felt ears in half and glue straight end next to Sherpa.

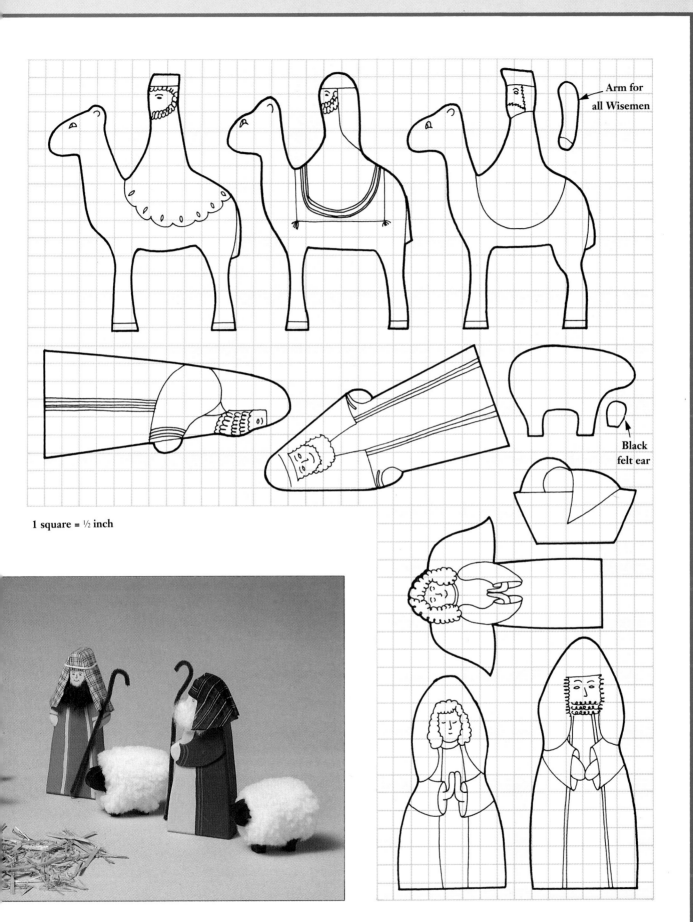

Arm for all Wisemen

1 square = ½ inch

Black felt ear

Sponge-Painted Wrapping Paper

Materials:

> 1 sea sponge, purchased at paint or art supply store and cut into 1"-5" sizes
>
> 1 roll plain wrapping paper
>
> Stencil paints in colors of your choice
>
> Pie tin or other paint container

Directions:

1. Cover table with newspaper and roll out wrapping paper.

2. Pour about 3 tablespoons paint in pie tin. Dab one side of sponge in paint and blot on newspaper.

3. Beginning at one end of roll of paper, dab sponge randomly over paper, applying paint continuously and in even pattern to end of roll.

4. Let dry. Apply second color of paint with different sizes of sponge as desired.

Note: Tree design on top side of package (shown in photograph) was applied <u>after</u> package was wrapped so that it would be centered. Tree was painted freehand using blotting and wiping strokes with sea sponge. Other variations include snowmen, wreaths, or bows painted on after all paint has dried. For a coordinated look under your Christmas tree, match paper and paint choices to colors and designs in your room.

Victorian Treasures

Touch Another Time

The traditions of yesterday reach out to us today.

In the evening, the Victorian mother sat in her chair, perhaps making a beaded firescreen, a papier-maché tray, or a shellwork box. The hands of the Victorian woman were expected to be busy ones, and she welcomed the opportunity to express her personality through beautiful creations. Today, not just mothers but the entire family can feel the spirit of creativity. Tree ornaments in lovely jewel tones mean more when they're made at home. Ornaments of doily and cross-stitch lend elegance to any setting. Homemade crafts have never really gone out of style, and these ideas for festive creations in the new Victorian spirit are fun for all ages.

Jewel Tree

Imagine sapphires, rubies, and emeralds hung from evergreen boughs, their many facets reflecting and multiplying golden Christmas lights. A plain fir tree is transformed into a majestic vision of gold lace, luxuriant tassels, and luminous pearls. You don't need a king's ransom in gems to create a jewel-toned tree, because the ornaments that follow can be made by hand from items readily available. The Jewel Tree is an exuberant reinterpretation of Victorian Christmas for those who love a tree that is a romantic vision of times past.

Faux Finish Frame

Materials:

1 piece 10" x 17" posterboard

Faux finish kit, or faux wallpaper or
    giftwrap paper

½" gold lace, 24 inches

1/16" gold twist cord (outside of frame), 36 inches

1/16" gold twist cord (inside of frame), 12 inches

1/16" gold twist cord (hanger), 5 inches

1 photograph 2¼" x 3½" (approx.)

Gold tassel, 3"

Oval pattern

Utility knife

Needle and white thread

White glue

Directions:

1. Decorate the posterboard using a finishing kit or by gluing on wallpaper or giftwrap.

2. Cut two frames from the faux-finished board using oval pattern.

3. To create a pattern for the center opening, measure the height and width of the portion of the photo that needs to appear in the opening. Draw this measurement on scrap paper and cut out. This is your pattern for the inside opening. Place this pattern on the wrong side of one frame and trace. Using a utility knife cut out center of frame.

4. Glue hanger on the wrong side of the frame back at the top.

5. Glue the tassel hanger on the wrong side of the frame front at the bottom.

6. Sew a gathering thread along one long side of the lace. Gather up until the lace fits around the outside of the frame. Glue the gathered edge on the wrong side of the frame back, allowing the lace to extend beyond the frame edge.

7. Glue the photo to the wrong side of the frame front, so that the photo shows through the opening. Trim the inside edge of the photo opening with 1/16" cord.

8. Glue the wrong sides of the frame front and the frame back together. Finish the outer raw edge of the frame with a 1/16" cord on both front and back.

Heart with Pearls

You may purchase a balsa wood heart box with lid, which is available at most craft shops. Separate the box from the lid. Cut cardboard to fit each heart shape, proceed with step #3, and you will have two hearts.

Materials:

1 piece 12" x 1" medium weight cardboard

1 piece 10" x 5" medium weight cardboard

Large heart pattern

1 piece 10" x 15" red satin fabric

1 piece 24" x 2" red satin fabric

1 piece 10" x 5" low-loft batting

3/8" red sequin braid, 25 inches

¼" ribbon, iridescent ecru
    with gold edging, 12 inches

¼" red satin ribbon, 9 inches

1/8" small seed pearls, approx. 100

10" wire for stringing
    (must fit through holes of pearls)

6" gold mini cord (for hanger)

Large heart pattern

Electric glue gun and glue sticks

Small heart pattern

Needle and red thread

White glue

Masking tape

Directions:

1. Cut two hearts from the 10" x 5" cardboard using Large Heart Pattern.

2. Fold 12" x 1" strip of cardboard in half and attach to the edge of one cardboard heart at right angles. The fold is placed at the bottom point of the heart and the ends go up to the top dip of the heart. Trim the ends if necessary. While holding the side in position, run a bead of hot glue on the inside of the seam.

3. Attach the second cardboard heart to the other side of strip, making a three-dimensional heart.

4. Using Large Heart Pattern, cut two hearts from 10" x 5" piece of fabric. Using Small Heart Pattern cut two hearts from the 10" x 5" batting.

5. Take 24"x 2" strip of fabric and sew a gathering thread 3/8" in from edge on both sides of the strip. The space between the gathering stitches should be 1 1/4" wide.

6. Gather both threads at the same time until gathered strip fits the 1" strip of cardboard around the heart. Glue one end (raw edge) down at the bottom point of heart. Fold under the other raw edge end and glue down covering the first raw edge for a finished look. Glue the gathered raw edges onto the front and back of the heart adjusting the gathers and keeping them taut.

7. Glue batting on both sides of the heart. Batting should be end up 3/8" smaller than cardboard heart.

8. Place fabric heart on top of batting. Glue only the outer 1/8" of heart fabric to the base. DO NOT OVERGLUE. DO NOT GLUE CENTER OF HEART. Use a toothpick to dot the glue at the edge of the batting on the gathered edge. Press edge of top heart into glue with a clean toothpick. Take your time and keep your fingers clean of glue.

9. Glue sequin braid in a heart shape covering the raw edges of fabric on front and back of heart. Start at the bottom point, proceed to the top, return to the bottom point. DO NOT CUT at this point but proceed to the back side crossing bottom of 1" edge and

repeat on back of heart as on heart front.

10. Cut one 6" piece and one 4" piece of stringing wire. String each with pearls. Secure the pearls at the end by bending the wire back and reversing it through the hole of the second pearl from the end. Fold the 6" piece in half. There will be 3 lengths: two 3" tails and one separate 4" tail. Attach the 4" piece by twisting at the fold of the 6" piece. Glue the three pearls' tails at the top of the heart, tails pointing downward.

11. Fold 1/4" red ribbon in half. Glue over pearls at top of heart. Cut the ends of the ribbon on an angle.

12. Tie 1/4" ecru ribbon in a bow with 1" loops and glue over the 1/4" ribbon. Cut ends of ribbon on an angle.

13. Attach mini-cord hanger to wire loop at top.

Jewel Ball with Beaded Tassel

Materials:

3" Styrofoam ball® covered with gold thread, 1
    OR
3" Dylite Styrofoam ball®, gold paint,
    and applicator

#20 gold wire (loop), 4 inches

1/4" blue crystal beads, approximately 86

1/4" gold beads, approximately 56

1/16" gold beads, 3

Gold beading pins, approximately 142

1/4" blue round jewels, 16

1/4" gold braid, 46 inches

1/16" gold twist cord (hanger), 8 inches

1" x 1 1/4" oval metal shapes (gold), 4

1 1/2" round metal shape (gold), 1

Needle and blue thread

White glue

Straight pin

Directions:

1. If required, paint the Styrofoam ball and allow to dry throughout.

2. Form wire into 1/4" loop by wrapping around a pencil and twisting the tails twice. Insert the tails into Styrofoam ball and secure with glue. Glue round metal shape at bottom, opposite the wire loop.

3. Visually divide the ball into four vertical sections

and glue ¼" braid from top loop to the bottom metal shape, creating three sections.

4. Beads are attached with a drop of glue and a beading pin. Starting with section #1, follow inside edge of the braid and pin and glue gold beads down to the bottom. Continue back up to meet the first bead. Inside edges of braid will be bordered by the gold beads. Do the same on the opposite section (Section 3).

5. Using crystal beads, repeat step #4 completing the other two sections (sections 2 & 4).

6. Toward the top of each section, glue an oval metal shape. Glue a jewel in the center of each metal shape.

7. Form three lines of braid, below the metal shape, to the bottom. Glue a jewel at the top of each braid line. Repeat in the remaining three sections.

8. Secure ¹⁄₁₆" bead at end thread to serve as an anchor and thread a string of beads using 12-14 beads. Repeat, making two strings of crystal beads and one of gold. With thread, tack the three strings together. Push straight pin through the thread, tack and attach the three strings to the bottom of the ball. Secure with glue.

9. Attach cord hanger to the wire loop at top of ball.

Note: Use a photocopy machine to enlarge patterns for Jewel tree ornaments 200%.

Nosegay Bouquet Ornament

Materials:

Plastic bouquet form, 3" diameter

Lace, 1½" wide, ½ yard

Green Styrofoam®, 1" cube

Greens

Prairie grasses or other filler

Statice

Nuts

Cinnamon sticks

Dried rose

Hot glue

Directions:

1. Gather lace and glue to edge of bouquet form. Glue cube of Styrofoam in center of holder.

2. Glue greens and prairie grasses or other filler in circle at base of cube. Arrange cinnamon sticks and glue in place. Glue nuts to top of cube.

3. Glue rose to center of cube. Fill any bare spots with statice and more filler.

Cotton Angels and Wonderful Santa

Victorian Cotton Batting Figures

Materials:

Cotton batting, Christmas tree skirt or quilt batting

Wooden craft stick, 1 per figure, ¾" x 6"

Printed angel or Santa face, purchased or cut from Christmas card, approximately 1" wide by 1½" long. See ordering information below.

Gold wings, approximately 2" x 3", cut from craft paper or purchased. See ordering information below.

Chenille stem, 12" long, 1 per Santa figure

Gold metal star-shaped studs (available at fabric stores)

Gold cord for Santa's waist

Trims, such as twigs, small pinecones, cloves, gold stickers, and greenery (ericmoss)

Antique stain made from 1 teaspoon instant coffee and 1 cup hot water

White craft glue

White sewing thread

Ordering information: For Victorian reproduction paper goods such as faces and wings, contact Gerlachs of Lecha, PO Box 213, Emmaus, PA 18049.

Directions for Angel

Note: Use glue sparingly throughout so that it does not soak through batting to the right side.

Body:
1. Cut a piece of batting 7" square.
2. Run bead of white glue down center of craft stick. Lay stick, glue side down, on one edge of the batting. Firmly wrap batting around stick. Secure loose end with glue; this creates a padded body.
3. Put dab of glue near end of stick, attach face and let dry.

Hood:
1. Cut square 6½ inches. Fold diagonally into triangle.
2. Put dab of glue on back side of padded stick opposite where face is glued and attach large corner of triangle with corner pointing down. Bring two loose ends around to front and glue under chin.

Coat:
1. Cut piece of batting 14" x 11".
2. Fold down 3" along one longer edge. Fold same edge again in other direction 2". This forms rolled collar, with raw edge hidden.
3. Run bead of glue down center of body under face. With collar under chin, start wrapping firmly but not tightly around body until finished. Piece should wrap around stick twice and finish near center in front. Fold any excess batting under for smooth center front and secure with glue. Front of collar can be folded down and glued slightly on angle away from chin.

Arms:
1. Cut a piece of batting 11" x 3½".
2. Fold longer edge down 1", then fold opposite longer edge up 1" to create long skinny tube. Secure loose edges with glue.
3. Find center of tube. Gather at center and glue under collar on backside of angel.
4. Bring arms to front on each side with ends touching.
5. Cut square 3½" x 3½". Fold 1 inch in on left and right side to make tube. This piece is laid over center where arms meet in front to create muff. Tuck loose ends of muff behind hands and glue all pieces in place.

Decorations:
1. Glue wings between inside of collar and back of hood.
2. Tuck greenery in front tucked inside tops of arms and around face, as desired. Cloves or gold stickers can be glued on front like buttons.
3. A gold cord hanger may be sewn through batting near back of head.

Instructions for Santa

Body: Same as for angel.
Legs:
1. Lay padded craft stick over center of chenille stem, 1" from bottom of craft stick. Bring one end of chenille stem around each side of craft stick and twist chenille stem tightly around itself twice. Fold each end in half back toward craft stick. This forms base for legs. Bend last ¾" of each end at right angles to form feet.
2. Tear 3" square of batting (do not cut; cut edges will not blend as nicely). Cover one leg and foot with glue. Wrap batting around pipe cleaner, folding in loose end around toe. Secure end with glue. Repeat for other leg. Brush finished legs and feet with a solution of half glue/half water to create a stiff coating. Allow to dry.
3. To antique, mix a solution of 1 teaspoon instant coffee to 1 cup hot water. Let cool, and spray from spray bottle.

Arms:
1. Cut piece of batting 15" x 3½".
2. To make cuffs, fold 2" toward center on each of narrow ends. Fold 1" of folded area back toward center on each end.
3. Fold one longer edge down 1", then fold opposite longer edge up 1" to create long skinny tube. Secure loose edges with glue.
4. Find center of this tube. Gather at center and glue under the collar on backside of Santa.
5. Bring the arms to front on each side with cuffs meeting. Glue cuffs together where they meet. Position arms as you like and glue to body.

Hat:
1. Cut piece of batting 4½" x 4".
2. Fold over double-thickness band ¾" deep on one long edge. Fold hat in half with right side of band together. Sew short edges together with ¼" seam, curving seam towards fold. Trim excess. Turn hat to right side.
3. Attach gold star to band.
4. Slip hat over padded stick head and attach with glue, centering seam on back of head. Glue top of collar and base of hat together.
5. Add clove buttons and glue twigs through arms, as desired. Tie gold cord around waist.
6. Sew gold cord for hanging through padding on back of stick. Knot ends.

Doily Crafts

Doily Ornaments

Materials:
   Doilies (gold, silver, or white) in various sizes
      (6½", 8½", 12", 14½")

   Glue gun

   Scissors

   Spray paint (if using white doilies)

   Baby's breath

   Florist's wire

2. Roll remaining piece into cone.
3. Using glue gun, glue sides together lightly.
4. Attach ribbon bow and small cluster of ribbon roses.
5. Attach ribbon loop for hanger.

Fan
1. Cut doily in half.
2. Using an accordian pleat, pleat to create fan.
3. Glue bundle of silk flowers to top.
4. Bend stem of flower bouquet to attach to branch of tree.

Nosegay
1. Pierce silk rose in center with florist's wire and pass through doily. Tie knot at end so it won't slip through.
2. Loosely gather doily around rose by hand.
3. Tie satin ribbon around remaining length of wire beneath doily.
4. Attach to tree with end of wire.

Paper Scrap Ornament
1. Cut Victorian Figures and faces from scraps of wrapping paper.
2. Glue individually to doilies.
3. Glue loop of satin ribbon to back for hanging.

Doily Decorating Trims

Materials:

> Assorted doilies, as above
>
> Glue gun
>
> Scissors
>
> Spray paint
>
> Gold foil wrapping paper
>
> Paper gift tags or place cards
>
> Gift ribbon
>
> Miniature silk roses

Directions:
1. For packages, wrap box in plain foil paper.
2. Run finger along edge of box to create crisp outline.
3. Make miniature of one of ornaments described above and place on top of package.
4. Glue scrap of doily to plain white gift tag and attach to package as desired, using ribbon as shown in photograph.
5. Use left-over doilies to line potpourri containers and as borders for picture frames.

Large silk roses

Narrow satin ribbons

Paper scraps of Victorian figures and faces
    (purchased at gift or stationery store)

Ribbon roses

Tiny silk nosegays

Directions:
Cornucopia
1. Cut wedge from doily.

Delightful Scandinavian Designs

Such simple-to-create charm

Wheat, whimsy, and red ribbon can become a part of your holiday traditions.

At threshing time, Swedish farming families always remember to save a sheaf of wheat to set out for the birds on Christmas Eve. That tradition of sharing earth's bounty is expressed in crafts that use the natural beauty of wheat to brighten winter homes. After you discover the versatility of wheat, you'll find your own ways to braid or fan its stalks. Then let the whole family help make an apple tree hung with American gingerbread men or Swedish pepparkakor cookies. For young holiday helpers, we've included woven paper hearts to fill with goodies or hang on the tree. They'll soon learn that homemade crafts express the heart of Christmas happiness.

Apple Tree

Materials:
 Wood
 Straight stock 1¾" x ½" x 36"
 Ranch stop 1⅜" x ⅜" in the following lengths: 24", 22", 20" and 18"
 Wood stain
 Small nails
 Plaster of paris
 Five pound coffee can or similar container
 Basket to fit over container
 Excelsior
 Wheat and ribbon for decoration

Directions:
1. Cut points on one end of straight stock and on both ends of each piece of ranch stop.
2. Stain all wood and allow to dry.
3. Mix plaster of paris according to directions on package and fill coffee can.
4. Push non-pointed end of straight stock into the center of plaster of paris. Prop wood so that it will remain upright until plaster of paris is thoroughly set.
5. Center shortest length of ranch stop directly below the point on the straight stock with the straight side of the ranch stop at top. Attach with two small nails. Attach the remaining lengths equally spaced along the straight stick.
6. Place can inside basket and cover plaster of paris with excelsior. Decorate with wheat and ribbon, as desired.

Straw Heart Ornament
Pictured above

Materials:
 Wheat straw with heads, 12 straws
 Raffia, 1 yard

Directions:
1. Soak wheat for 30 minutes to make pliable.
2. Tie 6 straws together with raffia under the heads. Hold tied end tight in a clamp or hook over a nail. Divide straws into two groups of 3 straws each. Twist one group over the other to create a twisted rope for 6 inches. Leave 2½" untwisted. Repeat with remaining 6 strands of straw.
3. Tie the two ropes together where twisting ends.
4. Bend the two ropes down in a heart shape with the untwisted straw as a center post. Tie with raffia at bottom. Trim off any excess straw.

Simple Shapes for Easy Ornaments

Satin Hearts

Materials:

Red fabric, 4" x 18"

Red ribbon, 1 yard of ¼" width

Stuffing

Matching sewing thread

Directions:
1. Cut 4 hearts. With right sides together and leaving an opening for turning, join two hearts using a ¼" seam. Clip seam. Repeat with remaining 2 hearts.
2. Turn hearts to right side and finger press seam. Fill hearts with stuffing and slipstitch openings.
3. Cut one 18" length of ribbon and tack one end to each heart. Tie two small bows with remainder of ribbon and tack one to each heart.

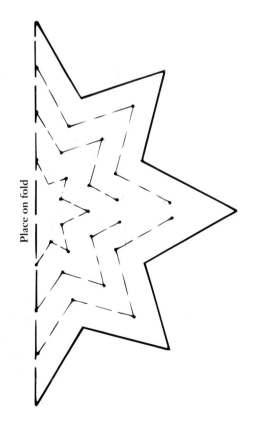

Cut 4

Clip seams before turning

¼" seam

Leave open to turn

Paper Star

Materials:

White paper, 4½" square per star

Invisible thread for hanger

Tracing paper

Directions:
1. Trace outline of half star pattern onto tracing paper. Punch a small hole at the location of each dot on pattern.
2. Fold 4½" square of white paper in half. Draw outline of pattern. At each hole on pattern put a light pencil mark on white paper. Connect the dots with small dashed lines as on the pattern.
3. Cut the outline of the star and along the dashed lines.
4. Unfold the star. There should be a connecting spine that runs from top to bottom of the star. Beginning with the outer section or "rib," fold one half forward along the spine and the other half backwards. Repeat with other sections for a three-dimensional star.
5. Thread a needle with an 8" length of invisible thread. Punch a hole in the top of the star with the needle and tie a knot in the thread for a hanger.

Place on fold

Woven Paper Hearts

Also pictured on page 100

Materials:
> Construction weight paper in red,
>   white, and green
> Glue

Directions:

1. For each heart cut two 3" x 9" rectangles and one 6" x ¾" rectangle.

2. Fold the two larger rectangles in half. Place the pattern on one folded piece. Cut the curved top and along the dashed lines. Repeat on second folded rectangle.

3. Hold the two pieces at right angles. Place loop A in between the top and bottom layers of loop 1.

4. Open up loop A and pass loop 2 through loop A.

5. Place loop A through loop 3.

6. Place loop 4 through loop A. Slide loop A towards top of slits.

7. Work loop B by passing loop 1 through loop B, loop B through loop 2, loop 3 through loop B, and loop B through loop 4.

8. Work loop C the same as loop A and loop D the same as loop B.

9. Glue the small rectangle in place for a handle.

10. To use the baskets as an advent calendar, print a number 1 through 25 on the point of the baskets. Place small gifts and messages inside each basket and present one each day until Christmas.

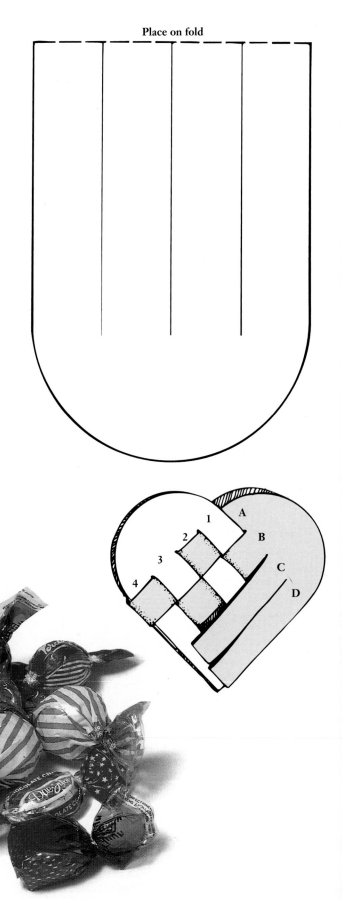

Place on fold

Nordic Kris Kringle

Patterns and instructions begin on following page.

Materials:

Red or maroon velvet, 9" x 24"

Black velvet, 6" x 24"

Green velveteen or felt, 5" square

Pink nylon stocking for head

Rabbit or fake fur strip, ¾" wide, 1 yard

Christmas trim, ¼" wide, ½ yard

Braid for belt, ½ yard

Polyester stuffing

Large seed beads, 2 for eyes

Gold star-shaped studs

Small jingle bell for cap

Gold thread for shoe laces

Curly sheep's wool for beard, 5"

Matching sewing threads

Directions:

Mitts:

1. Cut 4 from fabric.
2. With right sides together, join two mitts with a ¼" seam. Repeat with second set of mitts. Clip seams. Turn to right side.
3. Stuff each mitt. Whip-stitch tops closed.

Coat:

1. Cut two of red or maroon velvet with nap running down.
2. With right sides together, stitch seams as indicated on pattern. Turn under a ¼" hem on bottom of sleeves and around bottom of coat. Blind-stitch hems. Clip seams and turn.
3. Stuff arms to fill out.
4. Carefully push one mitt into bottom of each sleeve, leaving 1¼" showing. Whip-stitch bottom of sleeve to mitt.

Boots:

1. Cut 4 boots from black velvet with nap running down.
2. With right sides together, join two boots with a ¼" seam. Repeat with second pair. Clip and trim seams. Turn to right side.
3. Stuff boots firmly, leaving ¾" unstuffed at the top of each to insert into the body. Sew laces as shown with gold thread.

Body:

1. Cut 2 body pieces from black velvet with nap running down.
2. With right sides together and matching raw edges, baste legs to body at location indicated on pattern. (Legs will be inside body until stitched and turned.) Machine stitch over basting.
3. With right sides together, baste the second body part to the first. Sew a ¼" seam from neck down around bottom, being sure to catch legs in seam, and up other side to the neck opening. Clip and trim seams. Turn body to right side through neck opening.
4. Softly stuff body. Turn under ¼" at neck opening and slipstitch.
5. Pull top of body up through bottom of coat. Line up neck opening of coat with neck opening of body. Slipstitch coat opening, catching top of body at the same time.
6. Measure finished body to determine exact lengths of four pieces of fur needed to trim center front,

around hem and around both cuffs. If using real fur, piece strips together if necessary to form these lengths, being sure that fur texture goes in the same direction. To hide pieced sections and achieve smoother transition, trim leather ends of strips at an angle.

7. Turn fur strips face down and whip-stitch raw edges together to form long tubes. Fluff and separate fur; this also hides the raw edges and makes it easier to glue on coat.
8. Attach fur to coat with hot glue.

Face:

1. Use a 4" circle of pink stocking.
2. Run a gathering stitch ½" from edge in a circle. Draw up gathering threads.
3. Fill head with stuffing. Pull gathering thread tightly. Head should be approximately 2" in diameter. Secure gathering thread but do not cut.
4. Bring needle out of head on front of face at top of nose. Take tiny stitches around nose. Pull thread slightly to form nose. Bring needle up at "x" and attach large seed bead for eye. Repeat for other eye. Bring needle to back of face and secure. Come back to face to stitch tiny mouth; secure and cut thread.
5. Blush cheeks and nose with make-up.

Hat:

1. Cut one hat piece from red velvet.
2. Fold hat in half with right sides together and stitch ¼" seam. Turn to right side.
3. Fold under ¼" hem around bottom and blind stitch.
4. Stuff lightly to fill out.
5. Insert face into opening and line up seam of cap with chin of face. Baste head to cap all the way around. Sew hat and face firmly to top of Santa body.
6. Create a 10" fur tube in the same manner as described for the coat trim. Glue a portion of this tube over seam between face and hat. Do not continue around the back of the hat. Cut end. Glue remainder of tube around the neck to form a collar.

Beard:

1. Comb sheep's wool with a straight pin or pic comb and arrange as desired for beard.
2. Fold under loose ends at top of beard. Put hot glue onto wool and attach to Santa's face. Add a small curly piece under nose for the moustache.

Finishing:

1. Sew bell on end of cap.
2. Sew stars on bottom of coat.
3. For belt, tie 18" Christmas braid around waist. Knot ½" from each end and fray ends to create tassel.

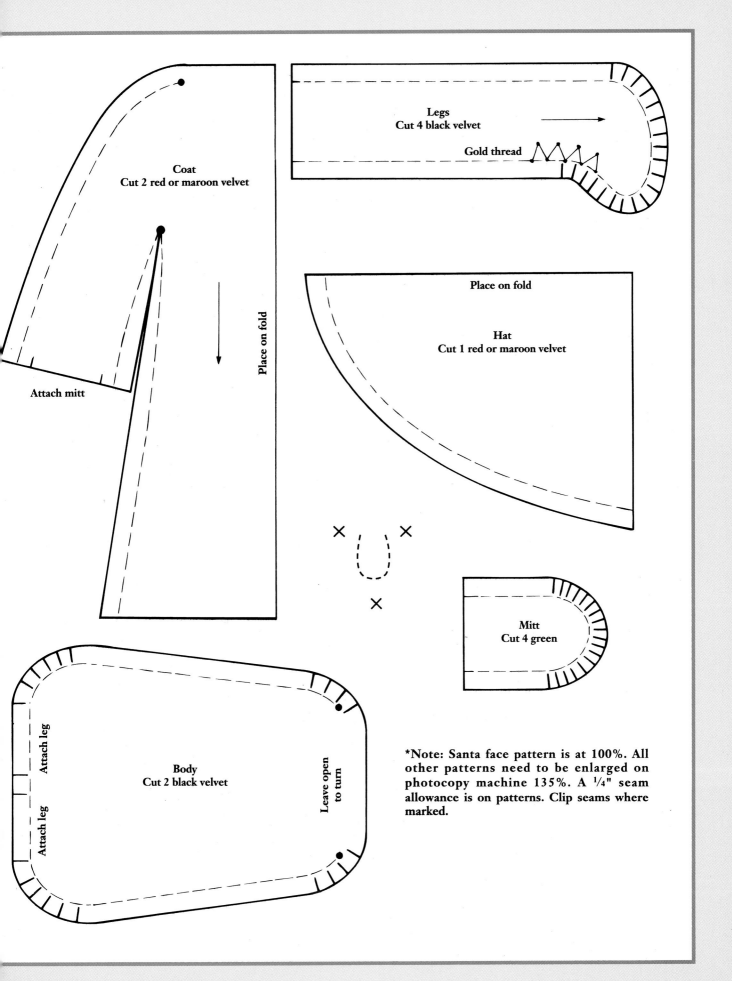

Coat
Cut 2 red or maroon velvet

Attach mitt

Place on fold

Legs
Cut 4 black velvet

Gold thread

Place on fold

Hat
Cut 1 red or maroon velvet

Mitt
Cut 4 green

Body
Cut 2 black velvet

Attach leg

Attach leg

Leave open to turn

*Note: Santa face pattern is at 100%. All other patterns need to be enlarged on photocopy machine 135%. A ¼" seam allowance is on patterns. Clip seams where marked.

Woven Wheat Wonders

Wheat Window Decoration

Materials:

    Wheat, approximately 75 heads

    Floral wire

    Hot glue gun and glue

    Silk leaves and greens

    Artificial berries

    Ribbon

Directions:

1. Soak wheat in water for ½ hour.

2. Gather stalks into a bunch with heads even. Wrap floral wire around stalks 2 inches from heads. Place on flat surface and fan heads. Allow to dry.

3. Attach wire loop as a hanger to back. Trim ends of all stocks even.

4. Glue the leaves and greens in place as desired. Add berries and bow.

Wheat Wreath

Materials:

    Wheat straw, approximately
        150 pieces with heads

    Metal ring, 5½" diameter

    Raffia, strand 18" long

    Heavy string

    Silk leaves and greens

    Artificial berries

    Ribbon

Directions:

1. Soak wheat in water for 30 minutes.

2. Lay 25 headless straws together. At the center place 10 straws, 5 with heads pointed in each direction. Tie all straws together at the center. (See illustration opposite page.)

3. Divide the straws to the right of the center into three equal bundles, left, right and center with the headed straws in the center bundle.

4. Work a hair braid by folding the left bundle over the center and then the right bundle over the center. Add 5 straws with heads to center bundle. Lock in by working left over center and right over center. Drop 5 straws from back of left bundle.

(Trim ends even when wreath braiding is completed.) Add 5 straws with heads to center bundle. Continue braiding, dropping 5 and adding 5 until desired length. Secure braid by wrapping with raffia.

5. Work second braid from the center in a mirror image of the first half. Divide the straws as for the first half. Work a hair braid by folding right bundles over center bundle and the left bundle over center bundle. Add 5 straws with heads and continue in mirror image of the first half.

6. Shape the braid to fit the metal ring. Trim off straw ends dropped on the back while braiding. With heavy string attach the back of the braid to the ring. Overlap the loose ends of the two braids and tie in the center with raffia. Trim ends even. Add a few extra heads at the center to fill in, if necessary.

7. Hang with a loop of ribbon at the top and decorate with silk greens, artificial berries, and ribbon.

Illustration 1.
Tie wheat together with heads facing
opposite directions.

Southwest Spirit
Symbols of holiday giving

These festive crafts will spice up your Christmas season.

Gilded cactus and evergreens, stars tempered from tin, chile-pods and gourds festooning a wreath, wrapping paper painted with cowboy hats and boots—let the myth and magic of Southwest tradition take shape in your hands. Spanish and Indian cultures combine to give these crafts a flavor all their own, from the warm and whimsical character of the coyote to the solemn beauty of luminarias. No matter where you live, this year wish your family and friends a Feliz Navidad with a handsome, handmade gift from the Southwest.

Luminarias

Materials:
    Paper bags such as brown lunch sacks or white bakery bags
    Votive candles
    Sand, potting soil or kitty litter
    Mylar or stiff paper

Directions:
1. Trace the outline of your pattern on stiff paper or the dull side of a sheet of mylar. (Patterns can be traced from books or magazines, or order pattern books from Dover Books.)
2. Cut out the pattern with an X-Acto knife, heat-tip pen, or scissors.
3. Lay stencil over bag, leaving room for the cuff at the top of the bag, and tape down.
4. Pour paint onto plate or blotting surface in about a 2" puddle.
5. Pinch the sponge to make a smooth, rounded end, and dip in paint once. Blot so excess will drip from sponge.
6. Lightly pat over the stencil, taking care over the small cut-out areas. Wash the stencil off when paint starts to stick to sponge so the edges of the stencil don't begin to curl up.
7. Let dry. Fill bags with sand, potting soil or kitty litter, and place candle firmly inside.

Pattern Ideas:
• Southwestern animals: coyotes, lizards, armadillos, snakes.

• Traditional Christmas symbols: stars, trees, candy canes, stocking caps, wreaths.

• Western themes: wagon wheels, cowboy boots and hats.

• Various shapes of cacti.

• Geometric patterns.

• Match stencil pattern to tile or wallpaper in your home.

• Coordinate with other Southwestern collectibles, such as pottery, rugs, or paintings.

Southwest Print Papers

Materials:

- Kraft paper
- Fine point black permanent marker
- Thin cellulose sponges
- Craft knife
- Heavy tracing paper
- Raw potatoes
- Toothbrush
- Pencil with new eraser
- ½" flat bristle brush
- Tulip Slick Paint Pens®
- Apple Barrel® acrylic paint
- Floral wire
- Hot melt glue and glue gun

Directions:

1. Trace patterns onto sponge or potato. For sponge prints cut out entire design with craft knife. Use marker to draw around design on cut surface of potato. Cut away all portions not to be printed.

2. Spread a small amount of paint on palette or plate. Pat damp sponge or potato (raw potato is damp enough to use as is) into paint. Spread paint with damp brush over surface of stamp.

3. Make test print on scrap paper.

4. Place several layers of newspaper under sheet of kraft paper to be printed.

5. Print designs about 1" to 3" apart in an all-over pattern. Begin with largest stamps and fill in between with smaller designs.

6. Allow to dry at least 30 minutes before overprinting.

7. Outline stamped designs with marker, and add Slick Pen details.

8. Allow to dry several hours or overnight before using.

9. Decorate packages with bows made from Creative Twist Paper Ribbon®, natural raffia, jute twine, yarn, or unraveled red burlap. Add accents of ¾" nickel conchos, small pinecones, pony beads, evergreens, or baby's breath. Wire or glue trims in place as desired.

Cactus

Cactus

Boot

Chile

Chile

Blanket
Triangle

Blanket
Diamond

Hat

Chile
Top

Indian Blanket

Coyote

Holly

Coyote

Star

Copper Ornaments

Materials:

36-gauge copper or tooling foil, 4" square for each star (You may have to order this through an art supply store.)

Steel wool, 0000 grade

Modeling tool, choose one with a smooth spoon-shaped end and a pointed end (Pencil or popsicle stick can be used instead of modeling tool if desired.)

Ballpoint pen

Liver of sulphur to antique the copper

Acrylic spray sealer

Tracing paper

Stack of old newspapers

Heavy duty scissors or tin snips

Old small paint brush

Straight pin

Directions:

1. Transfer design onto tracing paper.

2. Lay copper on a stack of old newspapers. Tape pattern on top of piece of copper. Using ballpoint pen or pointed end of modeling tool, trace over lines of design. Keep a firm but light touch while tracing to leave an impression in the copper. Remove tracing paper.

3. Using spoon-shaped end of the modeling tool on the back of copper, rub designs you wish to stand out.

4. Flip square over to front and work in indented areas using pointed end to refine and smooth out areas around raised areas. Repeat steps 3 and 4 until the embossing of tooling has created relief or three-dimensional pattern. Embossing can vary in depth; the more you work it, the deeper it will be. However, be careful not to overwork to the point of tearing.

5. Trim around outer edge of design using tin snips or scissors.

6. Paint surface of copper with liver of sulphur using an old brush and let dry. Lightly buff over raised areas with steel wool to bring out copper highlights.

7. Spray lightly with sealer. Using straight pin, poke hole in top of ornament to hang.

Trinket Box

Materials:

4½" x 3½" oval wood box

Three 1" commercial wood lamb cut-outs

26" white leather thong

Ceramcoat® acrylic paints—Burnt Umber, Trail, Green Sea, White, Avalon, Pthalo Green, Teal Blue, Luscious Lemon, Charcoal

Gold glitter paint

Aleene's Designer Glue®

Fine sandpaper

Saral® transfer paper

Directions:

1. Basecoat box and lid with white paint. Allow to dry and sand.
2. Transfer pattern to lid.
3. Basecoat lambs with Charcoal. One lamb should face left and two should face right. Allow to dry.
4. Dip a small wad of paper towel in white paint and "sponge" color onto lambs to give the effect of wool. Paint hooves with Burnt Umber. Set aside.
5. Paint foreground and hills with Trail. While still wet, load a flat brush with Burnt Umber and water and paint shadows in background hills using Green Sea and water.
6. Paint box bottom section with Teal Blue.
7. Paint sky on lid with Teal Blue, carrying color over edge of lid. Paint remainder of lid edge Trail. Recoat if necessary. Allow to dry.
8. Paint large star Luscious Lemon. Use tip of pencil or paint brush handle to paint tiny stars Luscious Lemon also. Paint cacti Pthalo Green.
9. When box is dry, recoat stars with gold glitter paint.
10. Glue lambs in place. Tie leather thong around box lid.

*Note the Copper Ornament patterns need to be enlarged on photocopy machine 200%.

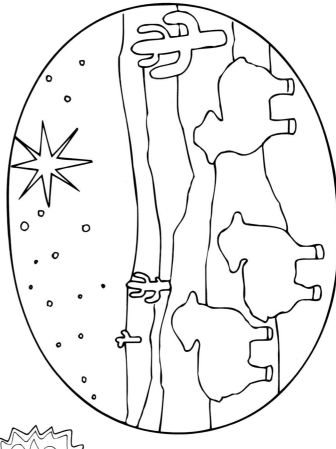

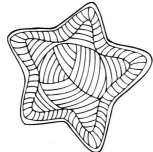

Painted Pillows

Materials:

- 14" square muslin-covered pillows
- ¼" masking tape
- Heavy tracing paper
- Graphite transfer paper
- Fine point black marker
- ¼" flat brush
- Apple Barrel® acrylic paints—Blue Stoneware, Victorian Green, Rose Bouquet, Straw, Berry Red, Christmas Green, Black
- Tulip Slick Paint Pens®—Gold Pearl, Black, White, Silver

Note: These designs were done on pre-stuffed pillows. The designs would, however, work very well on a flat surface.

Directions:

1. Use masking tape to delineate border by placing one edge of tape on seam line of pillow. Draw a line along tape on pillow front.
2. Trace border pattern pieces and cut out according to pattern directions. Pin to pillow and draw around with marker. Remove tape.
3. Trace center picture and transfer with graphite paper. Do not transfer lettering at this time.
4. Go over all lines with marker.
5. Mix paint with fabric medium following manufacturer's directions. Use color guide on pattern and paint picture. Allow to dry.
6. Transfer lettering with graphite paper and go over directly with black Slick Pen. Make dots on cactus on coyote pillow with Slick Pen.
7. Fill in large star with silver glitter paint. Dot in stars and Christmas tree balls.
8. Use gold pearl Slick Pen to dot in tree garland. Allow to dry.
9. Highlight red Christmas balls with white Slick Pen. Allow to dry.
10. Go over any lost lines with marker.

*Note: Pillow patterns need to be enlarged 150%.

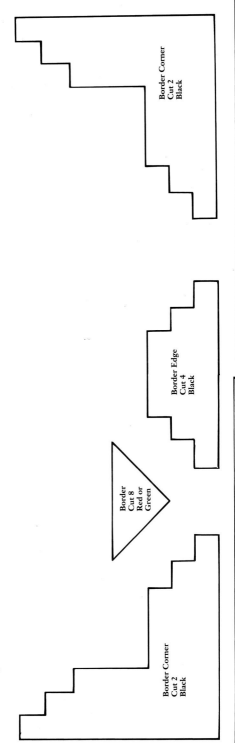

Gourds and Chiles Evergreen Wreath

Materials:
    Basic evergreen wreath, 12"-15" diameter
    10" velvet florist's bow (see below)
    8 gourds, spray-painted gold
    20 milkweed pods
    10 chile pods, 6" long
    6 ears colored miniature Indian corn
    10 fir cones
    3 yards #9 (1½") red velvet ribbon
    Hot melt glue
    Glue gun

Directions:
1. Using hot glue, secure florist's bow to top of wreath, covering ends of evergreen clusters.
2. Distribute decorating materials in a pleasing, balanced arrangement around wreath.
3. Glue in place with hot glue.

To Make Florist's Bow
Materials:
    Spool of floral ribbon
    #22 floral wire
Directions:
1. Cut end of ribbon at an angle.
2. Six inches from cut end, crimp ribbon and hold tightly between thumb and index finger. (Illus. 1)
3. Form a loop one half the width of required bow, keeping right side of ribbon out. Crimp and grasp with thumb and index finger. (Illus. 2)
4. Make an opposing loop the same size as first loop and hold. (Illus. 3)
5. Continue until bow is as full as desired. (Illus. 4)
6. Form two smaller loops, one on each side of center crimp. Cut ribbon, leaving a 6" end.
7. Carefully wrap an 18" length of wire around center of bow and twist tightly at back. (Illus. 5)
8. Gently twist and pull loops to fluff bow out.
9. For streamers, cut twice the length of ribbon required and wire in the middle. Add to back of bow, twisting wires together. (Illus. 6)

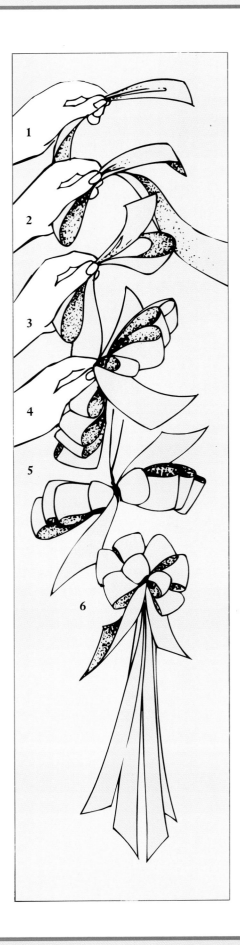

Christmas in America
A Time to Remember

For young and old, it's everyone's favorite time of year.

While the gifts are sorted and tucked into their new homes, when the tree skirt is folded and the ornaments are packed away in decades-old tissue, we pass around the last few cookies and store the tins in the back corners of our kitchen cupboards. Without the tree and those wonderfully familiar holiday decorations, the rooms look spare and just the tiniest bit empty. It's time to change the calendar as January's pink light lingers in the afternoon. And then we find a gift tag under the sofa, a pine needle in the corner, a bow still tied to the bannister, and the last few weeks come flooding back. It was surely the best Christmas ever, don't you think? And as we share our precious new memories, we can hardly wait till next year.

INDEX

ACKNOWLEDGEMENTS

Photography Credits

Page 5 Phil Shippert (top), Jerry A. McCoy (lower left)
Page 7 Phil Shippert (top), Michael Tincher (center left)
Page 18 (inset photo) Guy Hurka
Pages 24, 25, 26, 27, 28, 29 Jessie Walker
Pages 36-37 Lars Topelmann
Pages 38-39 Jessie Walker
Pages 40, 41, 42, 43 Guy Hurka
Pages 52-53 Michael Tincher
Pages 58-59 Guy Hurka
Pages 60, 61, 63, 64, 65, 67, 68, 69, 70, 71 Phil Shippert
Page 63 Scott Joliff
Pages 72-73 Huibergetse Photography
Pages 90 Jerry A. McCoy
Pages 110, 113, 114, 116 Michael Tincher
Page 112 Lars Topelmann
Page 118-119 Huibergetse Photography
Pages 18, 36-37, 40-41, 42-43, 58-59 were photographed in the Midwest Living Magazine 1991 Idea Home, cosponsored by the American Wood Council. Builder/Designer, Chris Baldwin; Interiors, R.A. Maxwell, Inc.
Pages 30-31 were photographed at the Hinsdale Historical Society, Hinsdale, Illinois.
Page 32 (left) was photographed at the Barrington Historical Society, Barrington, Illinois.
Pages 32-33 were photographed at the Dunham-Hunt Museum, St. Charles, Illinois.
Pages 64-65 Renaissance Green dinnerware courtesy of Fitz and Floyd, PO Box 815367, Dallas, TX 75381-5367.

Food

Food Stylist: Heather Hill; Photo Stylist: Carol Schalla; Recipes: Angel Biscuits with Ham Slices, Margaret Bartlett Torrence; Blueberry Cream Cake, Jean Roczniak; Hidden Valley Ranch Crunchy Pea Salad, Mrs. James R. Fisher; Sauerkraut Relish, Cathey Carey; Scandinavian Fruit Soup, Joanne Hultgren; Sing 'n' Sip Cider, Francie Graham Smith; Swedish Cardamom Coffeecake, Eleanor Baumner; Southwest Christmas Dinner recipes by Barbara Chernetz, Food Stylist Grace Howaniec.

Crafts

Crafts Editor: Susan Laity Price. Pattern Designer: Doris Schaffer; Crafts Photo Stylists: Sue Worthley, Carol Schalla. Project Designers: Copper Ornaments, Christy Crafton; Cotton Batting Figures, Christy Crafton; Cross Stitch Tags, Carol Krob; Doily Crafts, Carol Schalla; Flag-Waving Table Runner, Susan Laity Price; Gourds and Chiles Evergreen Wreath, Sandy Worth; Jewel Tree Ornaments, by permission of Diane M. Smoler from The Victorian Jewel Tree, copyright 1990, GFWC of Connecticut, PO Box 4284, Danbury, CT 06823-4284; Luminarias, Sue Worthley; Nordic Kris Kringle, Christy Crafton; Nosegay Ornaments, Lyn Creasman; Painted Pillows, Silver Romans; Papier Maché Country Crafts, Sue Worthley; Patriotic Centerpiece, Lyn Creasman; Quilted Stocking, Vicky Lumbert; Rag Sock Stockings, Margot Hotchkiss; Southwest Print Papers, Silver Romans; Sponge-Painted Wrapping Paper, Sue Worthley; Trinket Box, Bette Ashley; Uncle Sam Santa, Brenda Lewis; Whimsical Wood Nativity, Brenda Lewis.

Our thanks to the following homeowners who allowed us to photograph their homes: Walter and Suzanne Armstrong, Vernon and Joanne Hultgren, James and Linda McGrath, Joyce Miller, Lucy Sullivan, and Jerry and Sandy Williams.

In addition, we gratefully acknowledge the help of River Street Crossing, Batavia, Illinois; Father Bede, Marmion Military Academy, Aurora, Illinois; Baldwin Builders, St. Charles, Illinois. Special thanks to our Scandinavian friend, Joanne Hultgren, for sharing her heritage with us.